Back Like I Never Left

Dating as a Single Mother

By Rachel Wagner

Contents

"The only real love I have ever felt was for children and other women. Everything else was lust, pity, self-hatred, pity, lust."

-Adrienne Rich

4 my son

Intro

This book started as a blog. I was writing it because I was trying to just do whatever I wanted without thinking about academia or popular writing. What came out were stories about some of the dating situations I had going on.

At the time I was writing, only a small number of people knew the posts existed. It wasn't long, though, before some of the real-life blog readers I had started making me wary about what was worth leaving in or out. I could feel myself self-censoring based on who was looking. I could also feel certain dudes just wanting to be written about, which was weird.

But the real reason I lost interest in as a blog was because I knew I wasn't promoting it right. I was still fake scared about people reading it or saying I was writing it. I wasn't on social media at all (and hadn't been for years). I felt like I was just giving out content to no one for nothing. After a few months, I took all the posts down.

Looking back at this now, I'm just like, man what is wrong with me lol. But I know I was still learning how to be alone again. I appreciate my son for rooting me in something real.

Not Your Babymother

My first year being a single parent kind of sucked. I left my son's dad and stopped breastfeeding, but I still wasn't free. I would rush to work, hate work, then hurry home to my kid. I felt trapped in my own apartment each night.

It didn't help that the first few guys I talked to also sucked. They each reminded me why I tried so hard to stick with my son's dad. If they weren't broke they were ugly, if they weren't ugly they were lame. There was an ex who had nothing to offer emotionally, a local weedman who was too short for me, drunk men at a club on New Years breathing all in my ear.

Another was a married mechanic, considering a second wife (his wife knew about it). His intentions were clear—he liked me (how I looked and that I was in academia mostly), but he also didn't believe in leaving a woman who gave up her prime years to him.

Fine. I wasn't really crazy about the whole thing, but I was bored enough to spend some of his money at least. But before we even got a chance to go out or do anything, he just had to say something dumb. He told me while we stood in the poorly ventilated waiting room of the car place that a bonus for dealing with him would be that he loves kids.

I was like, "okay?"

"Well," he assured me, "a lot of guys out here aren't going to be into that, you know a woman with a kid."

And since he hated that I cursed, I told him, "men don't give a fuck if I have a kid or not."

Like nobody is going to fool me into thinking they're special for being okay with kids. Come on. I've met enough men in my life to know that they do not care about that. They'll take whatever they can get, and I didn't need to have a kid to know that. I'm not trying to play house anyway.

Meeting men used to be so different. It wasn't the sludgy, mostly solo mission it is now. It was something I did with my friends. Throughout the week, we'd be meeting or maintaining guys. Then we'd come together on the weekends and be like, "ok, what you got?" We'd all dig into our texts and compare and contrast before going with the best option. Does that sound fucked up? It didn't feel fucked up at the time.

It wasn't like we were bums. We had jobs. We were in school. We could go to a bar or restaurant or trip alone (and meet more guys). We were just looking for fun. And if the guys we chilled with were cool, then we'd keep chilling with them here and there to see where it went. It used to seem worth the night to chill with people we didn't really know because they might turn out to do cool stuff.

Needless to say, a lot of times they were not cool. We'd gotten stranded out of state, in screaming fights, pulled over by the police. Guys turning out to be ugly, guys who were disappointed that we weren't identical twins. A bunch of stupid shit.

Being thrown back in that exact same dating pool now has made me remember all too clearly the bullshit that comes with meeting new guys. Men just ain't shit, as a group. They think their little mishap is just that—a mishap. But they don't realize that they're ALL doing that shit at the same time, back to back.

Now that I'm older or now I have a kid at home (take your pick), I lose interest fast. I'm also just not as available, and maybe it's better that way. Now it's like, don't try to be spontaneous when we just met. You need to have a plan, and you also need to be a man that I specifically feel like seeing. I'm not rushing my kid around to see you day-of, and I'm not sending him off somewhere if you only have a two-star plan. There's no way I'm wasting a babysitter for anything even potentially mediocre.

Chilling at the House is Not Dating (but they know that)

Men are out here asking for house dates. Right now, in the continental U.S., men who are thirty and up think that offering to hang out at the house is an acceptable way to get through the proverbial door, just asking to be let inside [of you].

I've had more than a few new men offer this lately, so you know I'm not just talking shit. It's sad because people are doing this—letting men come over with a little bit of drugs and then letting them hit. I can confirm it based just on how many people try to offer.

At the same time, I guess I can't act like I've never ever done it myself (special circumstances, I'll call them). So I suppose if we've all done it once or twice, we've built up the ratio that makes them think that's enough. If they just go to enough women's houses or bring enough to theirs, a few are bound to fuck for nothing.

It feels like this was less of a problem

before for some reason. Are men trying to just come over now because I have my kid and can't really go out as much? Or maybe I was going to their houses more back then? I don't know.

There have been a couple times lately that I've let guys come over just for convenience, but I refuse to fuck or kiss or anything. Come if you want, comcast-guy. Bring ya stash, but you're leaving right back out empty handed. Really, coming over became the fastest way to ensure you were not hitting.

But that wore itself out fast. Using dudes for their liquor and weed and food in that way felt empty as hell because it was happening in my space. Got somebody sitting there with you, taking up space for no reason. You can tell yourself that doing shit like that is working with what you got, but what's really happening is the guy is being lazy, cheap, lame, and transparent about just trying to fuck.

A guy who I've known for years has been trying this maneuver a lot recently. He's always suggesting someone comes over—either *come over* or *can I come over*. And it's too bad because he's sexy as hell and is genuinely decent otherwise.

I reached my last inch of patience with him the other night after a full weekend of *come over* texts. I finally just told him he was bullshitting. You know what he said? That he was serious and let him know when he can come over.

Dude, obviously I know you're serious about wanting to come over. If anything, you're too serious about that. You need to either be a more interesting friend or a more active lover. And, either way, I'm not offering this pussy on a platter (or a couch).

Smoking Me Out is Also Not a Date

Smoking is automatic. I'm smoking with or without you. So the idea of getting smoked out by someone as a means of fucking me is like, huh? Don't misuse the weed. It's not an escape route from making a romantic effort. It's supposed to be some chill shit.

I can say that less people have tried this with me lately (trying to be nice here). And, yes, I know guys having been doing this forever. Maybe I'm sensitive to it now because it feels like a young, boring move. It's really not cool, especially when the options are either smoke with your dumbass or smoke by my own dumbass self.

A guy who lives near me just tried to fuck me after smoking a couple times. I always saw him peeking over at me when he saw me around. He was not my type whatsoever, but, hey, you can look. We never said more than hello to each other.

Then one day, we happened to be walking outside at the exact same time. He had a mild in his hand. I pulled out a clip. He said something like, "I didn't know you smoked." Then when I started to light mine up, he realized what it was. He said, "you blaze?" and pulled a fatass blunt out of his pocket.

So we smoked. Of course, he's asking me if I have a boyfriend and shit. He didn't say anything appealing the whole time but weed is weed. Took down his number and called it a day.

I didn't hit him up until I was about to smoke the next afternoon. He said he was about to go out too. So we smoked again. He continued to say extremely uninteresting stuff about whatever job he had (don't care) or if I was cool with fuckin with a guy who was in a relationship (ok, now you can really fuck off).

Immediately after the blunt was gone, I was thinking, *alright, time to lose him*. Just as I'm about to say I was going inside, he offered a drink at his house.

I was like, "a what? Nah, I have stuff to do right now."

And I really did, but also no I'm not going to your apartment for a drink. I'm not some unbeknownst teen runaway. Why do you think I'm going to stow myself away at your place for an ounce of hard liquor in the middle of the day?

Smoking me out counts as chilling. You get cool points for that. That's it. Hold on to them and keep moving forward.

On Longass Phone Conversations

I hate talking on the phone. It's is too much of a time commitment. I'd rather just text, unless it's something quick.

The other day, however, I found myself on a longish phone call with a guy I just met. I answered the call accidentally (an unsaved Newark number—thought it was going to be my son's dad), but the conversation was alright. I liked knowing that he wasn't a complete weirdo. I considered that maybe it was good to get the stuff we'd say on a first date out of the way (religion, why'd you break up with your baby's mom/dad, school). Now, at least, we wouldn't be complete strangers hanging out.

But when he hit me with phone call number two the next day, I was like, *ok I've got myself a caller.*

I was at a family thing anyway and didn't see it in real time. As I checked my phone with an expensive wine buzz, I realized that he was going to just keep on calling me every single day. And at that moment, I knew

I would not be answering. I have a million excuses, and I *will* use them.

I wanted to give him a little leeway because he's like twenty years older than me. And I don't care about his age. I mean, he signed every text message he sent me that week with his name at the bottom. Not even a proper text signature like people did for one minute ten years ago. Sometimes his was written out differently. He was manually signing his name after each message—and I accepted it! I didn't say anything about it.

But constant phone calls with no real-life action is where I draw the line. I see that as trying to put me on multiple pre-date phone interviews before really setting something up. I guess I had to talk myself into an actual date? Maybe it was meant to be sentimental, but I consider it bullshitting. Bye.

Is It a First Kiss If You Haven't Kissed the Person in a While?

My first kiss was when I was in pre-school with a kid who lived down the street from me. But my first *real* kiss—a kiss with someone I really liked and who I thought I loved—was when I was thirteen. We had no idea what we were doing. I remember our teeth clinking up against one another's, standing on my grandfather's front porch.

I recently had another type of first kiss. Technically, we've kissed before. A lot. I guess it's weird that I don't know when or how we first kissed years ago. It seems like it just started happening randomly and then we were doing it all the time. Whenever we turned up at the same place without someone, he and I would pair up almost automatically. But it's been a little while since then, like long enough for both of us to have kids, him to do a prison bid, and me to finish school.

Our second first kiss happened in the middle of a hot winter day. We'd been talking for a few weeks and hung out a couple times. That day, I happened to have an hour free at the same moment he was picking up. We were also five minutes away from each other, so we met up.

I kind of knew a kiss was coming at some point. But I was still in that phase that's like, *so is this guy going to make a move or what?* I love that stage, by the way, but I'm sure all Scorpios do lol.

When he and I first kissed again that day, I was reminded of my own body. It was like I was an inch away watching on. He felt like a new person. I mean, I was high, but it was still like a real first kiss.

Good Dick

Thinking about it throughout the next day makes your heart skip. It like droops down two inches inside into some deep dark space that you forgot existed.

That shit will have you hitting him up first or texting him in the middle of the day that *I'm thinking about your dick* or something like that. It can make all the shit I've ever talked about men go away. Come over. Smoke me out. Call me. Whatever.

People who really know me know that I actually love men. It's not all about sex, but getting temporarily dickmatized is definitely a part of the curse of being sexually attracted to men. I don't know.

Tinder Sucks Part 1 of 2

single mother
from jersey
reads
writes
fuck trump

That was my tinder profile for all of two weeks. A lot of guys were fake interested, but they were mostly bullshitters. It was a much higher probability than men in real life.

It's crazy because the app makes you feel like you're saving time—you can weed people out 1 2 3. You don't have to sort through live men or hurt anyone's feelings. You don't even have to physically leave your house. Suddenly, a bunch of good-looking guys in your radius come out of nowhere.

It would theoretically be ideal for a single parent who is stuck at home most nights. But it's not. All the scrolling, skimming, swiping. The terrible texting, the blocking of numbers. It's not worth it.

Nah, seriously. Why do so many guys put in their profiles that you shouldn't even bother if you're not a good conversationalist? Is there a certificate for that? And why are so many of these guys CEO's of companies that don't exist? That's a go-to move on the app that I'd never seen before—a guy pretending to own a pretend company even though he literally doesn't have a job.

It was also very curious to me that everyone was sharing their other internet profiles on there. For many guys, tinder seemed like just another profile to have. A lot of these guys' pages looked like business cards with their name number twitter snap IG linkedin BBM myspace soundcloud. *Damn, chill.*

And I don't have social media. I don't take a lot of pictures of myself. That's nothing I had to really defend before trying tinder. To these guys, not having a hundred shots of me in a variety of settings on a multitude of platforms ready to go meant I was probably catfishing.

More than one guy told me straight up they can't trust someone with two pictures up and no social media. Sending him a pic felt like a threat at that point. *I'll only talk to you if you send me seven .jpg images NOW* (I paraphrase). That attitude was weird probably also because I know I'm not catfishing. Hit me up. Spend some money. Make a move.

One of the first guys I actually talked to on there was cool. We texted off the app right away. He was like ten years older but went to the same high school and college as me somehow.

I remember spending time texting him while I was outside with my son at the park one night. But before I even got back inside, he admitted to losing his job recently and being back home at his parents. I respected his honesty and blocked his number.

Another guy I talked to was in Manhattan. He just moved there from London and was some kind of banker (so he said). I was reluctant about most NYC profiles because I already knew that I wasn't traveling out there for some dude. I mean, this is not ten years ago. I barely have time for local dickheads, let alone traveling for an hour for them.

He was cute, though, and funny.

Unfortunately, he brought up his dick within like ten minutes. I get that people want to hook up on there, but some guys are really logging in expecting to get their dick wet that exact minute. They're the ones who want to check and see if you're fuckin before making a gesture to get together. It's pretty gross.

I responded to him like, *yea this is why I don't think tinder is for me.* He said, *ok sorry I'll stop.* So he started asking me questions about myself. Two or three go by. Then he asked me what's my favorite position. Blocked.

I was overall unimpressed. Tinder was dumb. But even knowing that, if I got bored, I'd still be there swiping swiping swiping. You need to actually delete your account and the app to escape any website like tinder.

Instead, I began limiting my search to a five-mile radius. Talked to a few new guys. Mostly they just wanted to text, which I knew meant that they were in relationships. There was this firefighter from Elizabeth who wanted to text all the time. I think he was just bored at work. Blocked him after a few days.

Tinder Sucks Part 2 of 2

At the last second, right before I really deleted, I did meet up with one guy on there who lived nearby. I think it was just for good measure. He was cool, cute, all that. We got along, and he was generally nice. Not sure what more to expect by that point.

The dick was good too the one time we did it. But he got boring after that, just randomly offering to smoke. Bitch lol. No. I'm not fucking you for a blunt. Deleted the app and his number.

After him, I still had just one person left over from tinder in my texts. He seemed cool and lived near my job. We had just exchanged numbers. Talked about nothing here and there. He was cute and seemed normal.

He was another person who wanted mad pics. I was trying to tell him that we can Facetime. Whatever. I'm not hiding anything. But I sent him a picture of me that second, with a text saying that I look high as hell I'm sure. He was like, okay he smokes too, and *you look good I can fuck with you.*

Duh. Anyway.

So now you might think he'll act cool, right? Now that he knows I'm a real person? Wrong. He said something like, *maybe we can get together later tonight. My friend is having a house party.* The day progressed. The texts dwindled. The night passed. The next day he hits me up with the same shit—*maybe we should go out tonight.* I just shook my head. This fucking loser. I said, *lol maybe is your word.* Blocked his number.

I feel like anyone who is even into the emptiness that is tinder.com is probably a person I can't even fuck with. I've met okay men from the internet randomly, but zero from a dating site.

Unsolicited Dick Pics

Who is asking for dick pics? Please tell me. I want to know what you do with them. Also, do you just want the ones I get? Or maybe this phenomenon is just men's way of asserting their phallic dominance and so it has nothing to even do with what we want?

It seems like every woman I know has had a completely random dick sent to their phone. I remember getting a dick pic once from a number that I didn't know when I was like twenty-one. I told them to kill themselves, screenshotted the convo, and made it my BBM picture with the phone number left on it.

For those who are lucky enough to never received one before, it's not always a faceless dick in an alleyway. You may just as well know the person attached to it.

For some reason, guys run into it like an incoming train. Sometimes you can see that they're thinking about it. I mean, any attempt at sexting runs the risk of getting one. And I don't sext or do phone sex or any of that. See me in real life or get off my phone.

On the same note, I wish no one ever asked for another picture of myself ever again. If you want to see me, make it happen. Stop asking me for pictures. Stop stop stop. I've had enough. If we're cool enough, maybe you can take one yourself. Or I'll willingly send them to you when I feel like it.

I also sense in that picture question that they have a dick pic ready to go, and they're hoping to exchange. Like, they're asking for a pic hoping that you'll extend the first sexy pic.

I'll be polite if I like you and steer you away from there completely. The best thing that could happen is that they'll back off the subject when they sense that I'm not down.

Another possibility, however, is that you'll get one before you can even say you're not taking a pic right now. The guy who did that most recently was *this* close too. We were literally going to chill the next day. But he just had to send some dick pics smh. Now I have to ignore you.

Being Too Honest

My days of helping dudes out are over. Guys expecting or even requesting free labor from me are really fucking up. In no way am I trying to put in work for you—a ride, a therapy session, nothing.

The other day, a guy I'm friends with asked if I would write something up for him, and I told him no I don't write for free. He told me that I was being mean. I told him I was just being honest. He said I was too honest.

But really men are always asking for some damn help. The worst is those asking you to teach them how to show romantic interest. They want you to tell them exactly what to do how to do it when to do it. They don't care at all. It's just *give me the directions, and I might do it. Then kindly send along the next set of directions. K thanks.*

The problem is that it's too much work, and that's not you showing your genuine interest in me. My only direction is for you to have your own directions. Be cool by the time we meet.

That smokemeout dude confronted me the other night like, "damn it's like that?" I was like, "it's like what?" I knew he was talking about me blocking him after he tried to facetime me, but I kept right on walking towards my car.

To my surprise, he followed a few steps behind me the whole way. I could feel someone behind me, and I was telling myself like, *no wouldn't he just say something to stop me instead of being weird and following me? Maybe say my name to get my attention?* But when I turned towards my car, there he was, talking about what happened and why did I play him out.

I'm not going to give the whole dialogue here, but basically I told him he was bullshitting and he couldn't believe it.

He was like, "oh you're different" and "you must have gotten hurt a lot" and "so what was I supposed to say? 'Wanna go out Friday night?'" I was like, "dude you are out of touch. Anything would have been better than random calls and cheap house dates." Then he was like, "ok let me take you out." I was like, "nah I'm really good. Bye."

Dumbass. I mean, I wouldn't have said yes originally anyway, but at least come correct for principle's sake. I'm not doing that work with you to get you up to par. How you are now is who you are, and I'll just leave if I don't like it. I seriously don't have time to encourage men to do nice things.

But if you confront me in the street, I'm going to tell you about yourself for the sake of the next girl. Like please do better.

When the Wrong Guys Asks You Out

There's a feeling in the pit of your stomach, and maybe that's a good excuse to give him to get out of going—you're suddenly ill.

When the wrong guy asks you out, they usually know they're the wrong guy already. Whether there's good reason you can't date the person or if they're just not doing the right shit for you, it's pretty disappointing. You know that it is just not it. The butterflies you're feeling are about how you're going to let him down instead of wondering what to wear when you get together. It's, *will I tell you no or just start ignoring you? Hmm decisions decisions.*

I had a guy recently say, "if I asked you out on a date, would you go?" Umm it's really not attractive that you're not confident enough to ask me out lol.

Men feign interest in me like that a lot. It's mostly an empty abyss—seems like it would be cool to deal with me if it was extremely convenient. More than one friend of mine has told me over the years that they'd like just one time (lol some friends).

But I need something realer than that. I'm not looking for one specific thing or trait or whatever. I just want the person to feel right. I guess them having sex appeal is a factor. Forwardness is a factor. Consistency is a factor.

Love Languages and Horoscopes

When I stop to think right away what my love language is, I'm not sure. *Words of affirmation, acts of service, gift giving, quality time, physical touch.*

They all seem intertwined. If you go down that list, at different times I can fit into different categories. I mean, women are givers. I feel like we don't ever choose just one. How could we? If a person needs things, we give it. If a person needs different things, we give those instead.

It just depends on how much will really wear us out after a while. You eventually ask yourself: is it too much work to love them in this way? Because I could be loving someone else in different ways and it not be so draining.

If I had to pick one right now, though, it would be physical touch. Guess I always just figured my sex life reflected me as a plain old Scorpio. Recently, I also found out that I have a cancer moon. That combination (sexual/maternal) could be why I have these passionate, emotional flings. It's not so easy to distinguish loving with physical touch from sex drive, especially when so many dudes just want to fuck.

In this individualistic culture, we think our partners are special. The idea that someone else might show the type of love I want (in the end, I want them all, all the time lol) can seem completely irrelevant. Instead, you ask yourself: but what do I do with *this* type? I already like something else about this person. How do I learn to extend myself even more?

He Likes Me I Like Him, Time for Self-Sabotage

The second I get what I think I want I don't want it anymore. I hate that. Once the intensive flirting and courting period is over and the real care begins, I don't know what to do.

That desire stage is just so crucial and then it's like, okay so you're interested, been showing effort, look good. But why do I feel weird when we're out together? Why am I lacing up my shoes? Why am I planning my exit?

Not Exactly Ghosting

If you fuck up, I'm probably just going to stop talking to you. And just because I don't voluntarily explain myself, doesn't mean it's ghosting.

Real ghosting happens before you even link up or maybe after one time of linking. It's me not talking to you anymore because I don't care to explain myself to you and if you don't make a real gesture then I don't care if we ever speak again.

This isn't the same as canceling someone either. If you get canceled, that means you did some wild shit and it's only wild because I know you so I'm going to tell you that I'm done with ya ass (at my convenience).

Coming back from being canceled or ghosted is not easy because I've probably already deleted your number, and I don't answer numbers I don't know.

I've gotten messages like *hey baby how are you?* from random numbers, and I will read it and delete it. I won't inquire about who you are or even think about it any further. If you did something dumb enough to get your number deleted, I'm not looking back.

Periods and Plan BS

I just had what was essentially two periods in a row. I finished my regular period like a week before taking a plan b pill. I know that's murky water, but the condom broke so I wasn't playing around.

When I got pregnant with my son, I remember thinking about how all the symptoms for pregnancy are the same as symptoms for your period. Why is it not clearer?! Cramps, bloating, headache, soreness, etc. It's all the same for every possible outcome. Why?

And what is that paranoia really worth? With a plan b pill, you start worrying like, oh shit why do I have cramps right now? A few days after sex? Fuck, am I pregnant? Then you remember that you took a plan b pill the other day.

This time turned out to really be just a little bit of bleeding but a lot of emotional distress for the rest of the month. It was the longest run of PMS in the world.

The last time I took a plan b pill, I don't

remember feeling as emotional. But this recent time was a lot. I was so worn out from being sad about every single thing. And I'm already a very emotional person, always in my head and shit. This had me googling: *why am I sad + plan b pill.*

I was also scared enough to take a pregnancy test because I was seven days late for my period. Then the day after I took the test and it was negative, I got my period.

A month of pure madness.

To Date the Weedman or Not

I think the hard math on weedmen is that half are actively trying to fuck. The other half are just selling weed (unless you're actively trying to fuck them). I've dated men who sell weed. Who hasn't? But I don't think I've ever dealt with someone that I bought weed from first. Not that I can recall at least.

I met my last weedman on the street. He was cool. He turned out to be the most energized, on-time, ready-that-minute weedman that I think I ever had. I will give him that. It's so hard to find someone that's not a bullshitter. And I've been on both sides of it—the reason they're late and the person they're late for. That's just how it is.

But if you can find a weedman who is always ready to go, hold onto that number because it's rare. I mean, I would hit this guy up just seeing if he'd be around my area at any point in the day (that's how used to bullshit I was—tell me *your* schedule). But he was ready that minute every time, and he delivered.

He also had absolutely no game. I've seen a number of guys who were like this since being single again. It's sad to witness men who seriously don't know how to talk to women. I remember him asking me one time if I had a boyfriend. I said no. He said, "oh we're going to have to talk about that!" I was like, "what else is there to say?" He was like, "yea, you right."

??????????????

I continued to deflect every semi-flirtatious comment or tone towards me every time I picked up from him, and he was still always just a call away.

But a weedman like that doesn't stick around forever. Eventually they change their number or clear their contacts or both. Or they move or they die. I mean, where do all the lost weedmen go? I don't even know.

He randomly didn't answer a text one day, and I never hit him up again. It was a good run. Sometimes that's all you can expect. Consistent, convenient, and with minimal sexual advances.

Why I Don't Talk Shit About My BD

Because that's my kid's dad. That's family at the end of the day, even if I'm not with him. I'm not going to run around talking shit about him.

I hate when I hear men dogging out their babymothers. It never doesn't sound misogynistic. I'm just like, *shrug* you're probably a sucky babydad one way or the other? I don't know.

Because really, why are you telling me, a person buying weed from you, that your babymother did some hoe shit? Why are you running around with that story sitting in your mouth? Not cute.

Whether or not I'm with my son's dad does come up a lot, even though it feels like it's been a minute since I left him. Dudes are always asking if we're still together or not. I'm like, "no, why wasup?"

I know they're just screening to see if he's waiting around the corner to kill him or something, which is understandable. But we're really not together, so that's all I say. I don't offer any extra information about it. Besides, I wouldn't bring him out unless someone did some seriously wild shit.

The real thing to gather from the fact that we're not together is: if I can get over him, I can get over you. I will move on with no problem. I will take my things and go no matter where that leaves me. And I'll be good too.

Do I Really Look That Young?

I walked to the liquor store around the corner from my house with my son the other night before going to see a friend and his kid in the number blocks. We passed three guys as we walked through the parking lot. One of them turned all the way around to be like, "hold up do you have a minute?" I looked back at him. He was cute, so I said, "uhh yea."

He gave me his number and then next thing he wanted to know was how old I was. He was staring at my face hard, waiting for my answer. I was laughing like, "I was just going to ask you the same shit cuz you look young as hell." He was like, "no, you look young." He was thirty.

Then walking out of the liquor store a few minutes later, another guy stopped me trying to talk. Well, he actually just started walking alongside me asking questions. The first of which was if I'm of age. I was like, "dude, I'm grown as hell."

He was setting up a date before we

even exchanged numbers, talking about ok we'll go here and here and you don't have to worry about nothing. It was just some regular fast talk. I was like, "mhmm."

Then as we're hitting the corner, a woman called out to him saying that his cab was there. She looked over at me, realizing he was trying to talk to me, and called out, "oh, nah. Come on. This cab is going to leave."

And shout out to her because that was the perfect exit out. My son and I just kept walking, hand in hand, while was calling out for me to still just take his number.

Oh yea—and I got carded at the counter.

In Retrospect

Liking someone can sometimes feel like a mix of drunken and tunnel vision. It can keep you blissfully unaware of how underwhelming a person really is for far too long. One minute, you're talking to someone who seems cool as hell. Next minute, you're noticing that they're actually void of character (or broke).

Losing interest isn't always a dramatic on/off thing. People say you're in a trance for the first three months you're with someone, but that whole process shouldn't take more than a month, tops. Those first few fun weeks can be really great, even with the wrong person, but, beyond that, you're being dumb.

Looking back, it's not that the person is different from before. It's just that now you can finally see them.

Men with Kids

When I got pregnant, there were a number of men who were personally offended that I was having a kid. I was surprised by how many dudes really said to me, "oh I wanted you to have my kid!" Dude, what? Lol. I had sex with you a couple times like two years ago. You're lucky I still even respond to your texts sometimes.

Meanwhile, I didn't really care what any of them had to say because I was done. I'd been dating for years—like ten by then. I knew as good as anyone else that there wasn't anything out there. Actually, the last dude I met before I got serious with my son's dad literally drugged me (and P.S. I would have done the ecstasy if you would have just offered it to me, bozo).

So when I had the chance at an actual family situation, especially after that, I went for it (re: my cancer moon). I cut off everyone. I took no numbers. I set sail, never to return.

Maybe that's why I used to feel weird

about dating a guy who had kids—because I there would always be a whole family unit that would come before me no matter what. Whether they had one kid or nine kids, me and our relationship would always be secondary to that whole thing.

In the past, a dude having a kid was an easy reason to turn them down. I remember a guy pulling up to me on the street in Elizabeth years ago in a beamer with not one but TWO babyseats in the back. And he was genuinely surprised that I told him I was good.

There was only one guy I dealt with who had a kid when we met. Then we broke up and started talking again a few years later, and he had another kid in between that time. It was awkward. It wasn't that I wanted his kid, but it was like, so you really moved on in that time I see.

I'd still prefer a guy without kids (actually the most attractive thing to me is a guy who *wants* kids), but if a guy I really like has a kid or two isn't the end of the world. (more than that is the end of the world). But, yea, have a kid, don't have a kid—whatever. Just be cool and don't hover over me.

Tobacco Killz

I really hate when men smoke tobacco. Like it's not cute. I don't want to ever deal with that again. One of my exes smoked black and milds heavy, and I always hated it. I understood it was just because he was on probation and couldn't smoke weed, but then by the time he could smoke weed again, his tobacco addiction was already well underway. The milds never ended, even though he pretended to stop a few times.

And beyond general health and/or the wellbeing of the earth, when a guy smokes tobacco it also means he needs to step out all the time. Even in the cold. Even during a conversation. Being left at a table so a guy can smoke is not great. You know I'm going to flirt while you're gone, right?

Then they come back smelling guilty as hell. They return to you as completely different people. Fresh air and all. It's dumb (unless they have a blunt too).

A New Things Guys are Trying Apparently

The first time someone asked for social media instead of my phone number was at a house party in Roselle. It was a few years back already (early IG era).

This one guy I never saw before was half-sweating me. It was like he wasn't actually trying to talk to me, he just wanted me to know that I looked good. Cool.

Then he asked for my IG. I told him I didn't have one. He put his phone back down, kind of disappointed. He must have figured I'd have an interesting internet presence, so he'd stay in contact with me just to watch me. Um no.

—fast forward to the other night—

I was at a little event downtown, and two separate guys tried this other new thing I've never seen before. And it was one guy right after the other who did it. I really can't believe it could ever work. I mean, I thought the first guy was maybe drunk or something, but then the second guy did it. I was like ??

But, okay. They each talked or joked around for a few minutes with my sister and me before calling it a night and taking their phones out. Then they kind of flashed them at us like they were for sale, saying "you want to keep in touch?"

The question was asked to both of us or to either of us?! I don't even know. It was the most vague vague vague shit I've ever seen. And I love guys from Jersey, but I just have to say that a dude from NYC would NEVER.

It was just too easy to say no to because of how fake casual it was. So just either of us? Be in contact with you in any way? Huh?

I was standing there drunk as hell like, "nah, I'm chilling."

Chilling with ½ a Couple

Went to this bar the other night and ended up with two different people who were each an inch away from marriage. Oh, man. What a buzzkill. I couldn't even get drunk properly.

I'm even a hater, it's just when they get together, they're happy to not be alone at that stage. And, for me, it's just not fun. I feel like we're in school talking about Jane Austen. The appropriate time to marry, the best way to go about it, the different methods to cover up bad behavior.

No. I want the dirt you're covering with how sure you want to seem. What does he do that makes you want to kill him in his sleep? What has he bought you lately? Is he a freak?

And you already know everything you say to them is going in one of their ears and out their partner's. People in relationships are always telling each other everything. Especially when they have kids or are married. That level of legal seriousness guarantees any and all secret sharing. I know because I've done it.

Most people do that in the privacy of their own homes, but I've also had it happen right in front of me. The other day, I was telling someone something when their partner stepped away. Then when their man came back, they relayed what I said back to him. Right that second. Umm I could have waited until they were around if I wanted them to know what I just said.

Just Forfeit

I've had dudes fuck up bad as hell, then try to come back a couple weeks later saying they still wanna fuck wit me. Like, dude?? How long has it been since I saw you last *squints*. How are you still calling me baby and shit? How how how? Am I really still your boo after a month or two?

There's also someone who like it's been months—damn near a year. Bro, you can't keep a fence around me just because you hit one time. I do what I want.

In my eyes, if a couple days go by after fucking and the next thing doesn't get set up, I'm pretty much done with you. After that point, you can't say shit about who you see me with or who I'm fucking with.

That's the same way I feel about meeting someone new. You have only a few days to do something interesting with me or for me or because of me. A date, something. Once we start talking, get on it or get gone.

Being Someone Else's Compliment

I've seen that obvious nudge, stare-down, whatever a million times. It's not even directed at me—it's directed at the dude I'm standing with. There's also the subtle won'tlookatyou move these complimenters do too. Like dude won't even glance your way because you look mad good. But either way, it's not really for you.

I remember a while ago I was standing on the steps with this dude in the Bronx. I think one of his cousins was standing there too. I was wearing a schoolgirl skirt and heels and his uncle walked up the stairs shaking his head, saying the dude's name who just kind of just laughed. His uncle had barely even took a second look at me.

The other day, I was with this other dude in his hallway smoking. I had on a tight jean skirt and kitten heels. A guy walked past me and was like, "oh my god. Do they call you gorgeous snowbunny?" I was like, "yea I guess they do sometimes."

A few minutes later, a different dude

coming down that same little hallway was like "hello gorgeous" and then went up to the guy I was with and was in his face just staring him up and down saying, "your ugly ass." It was funny at least (these were all his family members too).

Regretting Going Out vs Regretting Staying In

The cold weather this spring has really been made it easy to stay in and not care. I have a young child who needs someone to be home to supervise his sleep anyway. Can't go anywhere unless it's planned for someone to take him, and a lot of the time, I'd rather just chill with him than go do something dumb anyway.

But as it inches towards warm weather, if he's gone and I don't have plans (like someone randomly takes him), I wonder to myself, *am I wasting my time by staying home and not doing shit? Or am I being dumb for forcing myself outside somewhere that I don't really even care to be just because he's gone?*

Or maybe I wasting time thinking too hard about what I'm doing or not doing? You know how in the summer you might randomly stop to check with yourself to be like, *am I doing what I want right now or not?*

How to Turn ½ a Blunt Into Like 8 or 9 Blunts

step 1: Go outside to smoke the rest of yesterday's blunt. See a guy outside smoking. Go smoke with him instead.

step 2: Go inside and put on a sexy ass dress.

step 3: Go to a spot with that same ½ a blunt. Go to the next spot with that same ½ a blunt.

step 4: Spark up right away cuz you're just coming from a non-smoking spot anyway and shit you haven't smoked since earlier so you wanna smoke.

step 5: Pass it to the group you're with cuz fuck it.

step 6: All future blunts and stuff

will come your way.

Rather Go 2 Your Place

I have an ex who acted like things were unbalanced because we went to my house a lot. But we were only at my house because I hated his apartment and liked having all my things around, especially in the morning.

But with just dating, I'd rather go to the dude's house even if my kid isn't around. I don't feel like showing men where I live, and, more importantly, I'm not trying to get trapped with you at my place.

I want to be able to leave at 2am if you're talking some bullshit. I want to be the one who can just leave. Because, man, that ride home is the opposite of leaving in the morning. It's not some ponytail and yesterday's clothes. At 2am, it's still today. I can still go somewhere else.

I took that ride the other night at like 3am and ran into a friend of mine a couple blocks away from my apartment. So we chilled and smoked at his place for like three more hours before I really went home.

Was great. Way greater than just

sticking around at a dude's place.

Hmm Could I Really Ever Date a Cop

No.[1]

---

[1] And even beyond their job, they're also usually dicks anyway. One tried to talk to me recently while I was struggling to get my tired and crying child into the car. The cop dude was grilling me with his cop friend from across the street. I could tell by the stare that he was going to try to talk to me. It didn't take long for him to kind of situate himself near my car. He was just talking shit, but it was all 100% about himself. Literally every word that came out of his mouth. Like ok give me your number just don't assault me.

So There's This Guy

Nevermind

A Lot of Energy

This dude who was not cute enough to be trying to come onto me came onto me the other day leaving the county jail for visitation.

My son was running as fast as he could down the ramp. The dude said something about him hauling ass. He was like, "where he get that energy from?" I was like, "I don't' know" (because I'm in my head like, *I know this dude is not trying it*).

Then he was like, "I mean is it from mom or dad." I think I said, "I don't know. He just got it from himself." He said, "I want to know if he gets that energy from you." I looked at him like, "yea, it's possible."

He got my attention because his shit got derailed like three times, and he didn't lose his cool lol. And he was dressed alright too. Drove an Audi.

Sidedick to the Sidedick

I hate the idea of rebounding. Probably because it's so obviously fake, and I like genuine connections.

In the past, I've had a few rebound guys turn into relationship guys because they stuck around as long as I'd let them. When I was a teenager, it would be like, *okay what's worse? The guy I finally left or the guy I ran to who also acts crazy?*

Part of rebounding is knowing it's a rebound. You're using another person to get over a relationship. I mean, sometimes it works. If the guy is generous, cool, and sweet, and doesn't really know or care if he's a rebound, it can be fine.

But rebounding doesn't always have to be so official. When you're just dating around and kind of interested in someone but don't really want to be, sometimes the best thing to do is to find another dude to fuck too as a distraction.

It's basically sidedick to the sidedick, and it borrows a lot of its elements from rebounding. Except here you have one favorite guy who is in the rotation, along with a couple others in order to avoid getting hooked onto anyone before you're ready. It kinda works.

Pretty Obvious Not to Follow Women in the Dark

I was walking around my block smoking a couple weeks ago, and this dude who once dumped a bunch of relationship shit on me fuckin followed me to my back door.

Bro, even if you're not going to assault me, you should know not to do that. But maybe he was going to assault me. Who knows. Still, I think most people know that you don't follow women to their door at midnight. Back the fuck up and go home.

I heard him call out for me when we were still about thirty steps away from each other. I just kept walking. I peeked back a couple times, and he was still there, walking fast as hell trying to catch up to me.

I had just got through chilling with a dude, so I called him to tell him what was going on. I told him he didn't need to swing back around necessarily. I just wanted him to be at least aware.

I slipped into my apartment as fast as I could and looked out the window to see where he was. Dude really walked all the way to the backdoor, which was closed by the time that he got there. Then he turned around and kept walking. What is wrong with you?!

Then like a week later, two guys followed me inside my building in the middle of the night. It was a Dominican looking dude and whiteboy who happened to be walking through my parking lot at the same time as me.

The Dominican dude kept telling me how beautiful I was. Yea, yea. The whiteboy was zooted enough to chase after the end of a blunt I threw. Actually, the first thing that was said to me was by the whiteboy asking if I had a cigarette, which I didn't. The whiteboy introduced himself with his eyes practically closed. The Dominican guy mumbled that he needed to lay off the xannies.

By the time I got to the backdoor, the Dominican guy asked for my snap. I was like, "don't have one—okay, bye."

The two of them proceeded to act like they knew someone in the building anyway, as if that's where they were going. I knew they were lying, but I also know better than to panic. I just nodded and kept going inside.

As I was rounding the corner of my hallway, they were standing around awkwardly in the little lobby area. The Dominican dude poked his head around the corner like, "can I get your number?" I was like, "I'm good. I don't know you." Then he gave me the old cliché, "I could get to know you." "I don't think so."

I got into my apartment, locking the door behind me. Again, I was happy to be home. I felt safe in my apartment and safe in my body because I know how to survive these interactions, but I hate that men feel so entitled to me just because I exist. They have no measure or concern for what's considered obviously creepy.

Men in Cars

The other night, this dude pulled up next to me in a gold Cadillac at a red light around the corner from my house. He was like, "you look like you're about sixteen." I was like, "what? I'm a grown woman."

He thought that was funny, but I could tell that he didn't like that he couldn't read me. When he asked if I needed some budd, I told him, "dude, I'm going to *smoke* weed right now. Not buy it." Like, you feel me or not? To me, that's plain English for: I'm not a custy, I'm a hoe.

Then a few hours later at like 4am, leaving from smoking hella weed with a dude in the south ward, I reached my block thinking to myself how deserted it was down the hill at that time—no one driving or even walking around barely.

A brand-new BMW truck with all the price stuff still written on it (like it just came off the lot) followed my car into my parking lot. I thought, *oh boy I'm about to die*.

I mean deep down I knew they're most

likely thinking I'm fuckable, and I know how to maneuver that to a certain extent. I'm lucky that guys don't see me and want to rob me or kill me right away. They mostly just want a chance to fuck me. So, whatever. I'll just play by those rules to get out alive.

Still, I decided to pull up closer to the cameras so that they could catch their license plate and stuff in case they did try some slick shit.

I pulled over and looked over. It was two guys in there. I rolled down my window like, "wasup." They were like, "you wanna chill?" I was like, "do I know you?" Then the passenger slurred out, "no but we could chill and have a good time, do whatever." I was like, "nah, I'm good." They were like, "ok can you let us out the gate." I was like, "YUP." Got their asses right out of there.

After they left, I parked my car and hurried inside. I was so glad to be home and also so sick of being alone all the time. Maybe I'm just sick of negotiating these situations. I'm annoyed that I'm good at it.

It's also annoying that when I tell people what happened, they're relaying all the things they would have done—called the cops, screamed out, drove away so they wouldn't know where I lived, etc. Like, you clearly do not understand the delicate balance it requires to play cool.

Men Without Cars

The only time I'm willing to drive is if the dude's license is fucked up. And even then, I need to be driving your car or there's no reason why we're even getting together. If you're a man, especially a man in New Jersey, you just need to have a car. No, rideshares are not cars. Either get a car or please don't talk to me.

Even if I didn't have a car either (which I do), why would I mess with someone who has absolutely no wheels? This isn't going to be some meet me here meet me there things. If you can't pick me up, I don't want to go.

This guy wanted to go out with me the other day and since I was already on the move (I think I had just dropped off my son off somewhere when he happened to hit me up to get together), he told me to meet him at this restaurant in the Ironbound. Okay.

So I got there before him and the place was closing. I walked back to my car to wait for him. He came and was like aw man. Okay let's go here instead. I'm like ok where'd you park (because he walked up to me)? Bro said he got an Uber there.

Hold up—what??

What kinda shit is that! I don't care that you can take public transportation to work and it's easier or faster that way. Like I really don't care about that information. Get a car.

Clearing the Roster

There are two main situations when you have to just clear the roster and start over:

1. everyone in your phone is being lame
2. you met someone who makes everyone else seem lame

In the first case, people aren't being fun as a group. Like their individual boring selves have merged together with every other guy in your phone to equal one big boring monster-text.

There was one Friday night that I had three or four guys in my texts, and each one of them had either a terrible plan or non-plan for us. I stopped talking to all of them after that night.

I also took a minute to clear out every name of a guy I didn't immediately recognize. The guys I actually knew stayed, but every conversation got deleted. Everything.

The other thing that might influence

that kind of restart is if you meet someone you really like. It's then that you might begin to feel compelled to be a lame person to others. Suddenly, they all seem ugly and boring because they're not the guy you actually want to be hanging out with. They make their little half-assed attempts to see you or do something for you, and you dip and dodge as needed.

Eventually, a lot of those guys will get the picture and just fade away. A couple stragglers might be hidden in the back, but that's about it.

Either way, I know that I need to be more straight in general. I've been accepting some men purely as entertainment, even if I don't like them that much. I have to do better.

About the writer:

Rachel Wagner is a writer and university instructor from New Jersey. She grew up in Cranford and currently lives in Newark with her son.

Rachel-Wagner.com

About the cover artist:

Lauren O'Hagan was born and raised in Bergen County, New Jersey. After four years of living in the DMV area after high school, Lauren decided to finish her degree in graphic design in Arizona. She currently lives in Phoenix with her dog Luna.

Laurenohagan.wixsite.com/portfolio

Made in the USA
Monee, IL
31 July 2021